BAKING SECRETS
from the Bread Monk

~

Tips, Techniques, & Bread Lore
2nd Edition

Library of Congress Control Number: 2022939693

ISBN: 9781681064154

Design by Nick Hoeing

Interior images courtesy of Pixabay, Unsplash, and Wikimedia Commons.
Many clipart images used throughout the book are designed by Freepik.

Printed in the United States of America
22 23 24 25 26   5 4 3 2 1

BAKING SECRETS
from the Bread Monk

~

Tips, Techniques, & Bread Lore
2nd Edition

Father Dominic Garramone, OSB

Dedicated to my brother Marty:
I still look up to you.

Table of Contents

Introduction

I have found that you don't realize how much you know about a subject until you try to teach it to a beginner. After being involved with several cookbook projects with me, my publisher Josh Stevens of Reedy Press decided he would explore the world of bread baking and is now well on his way to becoming a full-fledged Breadhead. And naturally, as he progressed, he would call me for advice.

His questions spanned every aspect of baking, from history to ingredients to equipment to techniques: "Who discovered yeast baking?" "What is the difference between active dry and fast-rising yeast?" "How do I know the dough has risen enough?" "Why does my pizza dough spring back when I try to roll it out?" "Why are pretzels shaped that way?" "Why do I have to have unsalted butter?" "Dark pans or light pans?" And last of all: "Why don't you write a book of baking secrets?"

So I started making a list of things I thought different kinds of bakers might want to know. History buffs will be fascinated with bread lore about baking in ancient times (see page 5) and Marie Antoinette's fatal statement about cake (page 2). Beginner bakers will enjoy getting the 411 about mixing and kneading (starting on page 53), while more experienced bakers may want more about shaping techniques (starting on page 45), and everyone seems to need more info about "What went wrong?" (starting on page 67). I spent an enjoyable month researching food holidays (starting on page 87), and my fellow monks appreciated the opportunity to taste test my "mash-up" recipes.

I dedicated this book to my brother Martin, who is a reference librarian at Austin Community College. My mom would often call him when she couldn't find an article she remembered or wanted more information about a particular subject. Between her many years of baking and her extensive cookbook library, she had a treasure trove of baking secrets that she generously shared with me over the years. She passed away as this book was being edited—I will miss her expertise and encouragement. Barbara Northcott of Reedy Press also prompted me to expand my original concept into additional areas of bread lore and kitchen wisdom, and I am grateful for her assistance, as I am for Josh's continued support and encouragement.

And I am grateful to all the Breadheads who have been with me since my days at PBS and everyone who has joined our extended baking family along the way. I'm fascinated with culinary trivia, and I have learned many tidbits, techniques, and fun facts from you over the past decade or so, but your support and enthusiasm are anything but trivial.

HISTORY

Marie Antoinette Never Said "Let Them Eat Cake"

Most people have heard the story that when Marie Antoinette was told the French peasants had no bread, she replied: "Let them eat cake." In fact, almost everything about this "quotation" is inaccurate. The man who offered the quote, Jean-Jacques Rousseau, simply reported that he had heard of "a great princess" who, when told the peasants had no bread, responded, "Let them eat brioche." This buttery, cake-like bread, enriched with eggs and sugar, was commonly eaten by the upper classes and no peasant could afford it. But when Rousseau recorded this story, he was writing no later than 1769, when Marie Antoinette was 13 years old and living in Austria. Letters from the queen to her family indicate she was well aware of the plight of the poor and worked to alleviate it. Revolutionaries later attributed the remark to her as a means to discredit the French monarchy.

Egypt: The World's First Breadbasket

The earliest use of grain was for porridge and, eventually, flatbreads cooked on a stone. Six thousand years ago, the Egyptians were the first to make raised bread, using wild yeast or sourdough. They produced both barley and wheat flour from the abundant harvests of the Nile-fed fields, grinding it in small amounts at home but also in larger mills powered by oxen or slaves. The royal bakeries made bread in such large batches that slaves kneaded the dough with their feet in huge troughs. Breads were often baked in large ceramic molds known as *bedja*.

How the Ancients Shaped Baking

The Egyptians made loaves in the shape of spirals and cones and used molds to make bread shaped like animals. In ancient Rome, bakers began experimenting by adding ingredients like honey, fruit, and nuts, but they also shaped bread for specific occasions. For example, bread shaped into intertwined hearts was served at weddings. Bread was so much a part of Roman culture that in addition to small domestic ovens in nearly every home, archeologists have found more than 40 bakeries among the ruins of Pompeii. Likewise, a Greek historian writing in the third century AD lists 72 different kinds and shapes of breads baked for various occasions and levels of society. These ancient traditions continue today in the wide variety of flavors and shapes to be found at artisan bakeries around the world.

Medieval Monks Brewed *and* Baked

In medieval monasteries, breweries and bakeries were often situated side by side with a common storehouse because they used the same ingredients. In the *Plan of Saint Gall,* a medieval architectural drawing of a monastery from the early ninth century, this pattern is repeated three times, with separate bakery/brewery facilities for the monks, the guesthouse, and the hostel for pilgrims and paupers. The plan even includes the oven for the bakeries, which was round and situated by an outside wall. The *Plan of Saint Gall* is the only surviving major architectural drawing from the period between the fall of the Western Roman Empire and the 13th century.

Medieval Lords Used Bread as Plates

In medieval Europe, the lord of the manor was obliged to feed all the people under his care. In fact, the word "lord" is a corruption of the Saxon word *hlaford*: "bread giver." Meals took place in a large hall with a strict seating arrangement according to rank. It was impractical to have plates for so large a gathering, so cuts of meat were served on large, narrow slices of crusty bread. These "trenchers" (which became soaked in gravy and fat) were never eaten at the meal, but collected afterwards and given to servants or distributed to the poor. If you ate even this crusty bread, you were said to "eat like a trencherman."

When Slicing Became the Official "Best Thing"

Have you ever wondered about the expression "the best thing since sliced bread"? Wasn't bread always sliced? But in fact, the idea of slicing bread is uncommon in many cultures and is even considered disrespectful to the bread—hence the expression "break bread together." Bread-slicing machines were around in the late 1800s, but the loaves themselves were not sufficiently uniform to mechanize the process. Once machinery was developed to create uniform loaves, Iowa salesman Otto Francis Rohwedder invented the first machine to slice and wrap loaves of bread in 1927. This culinary innovation arrived just in time, too—in 1921, inventor Charles Strite had received a patent for the electric pop-up toaster!

The Romantic Tale of Pannetone

At Christmas, every Italian bakery sells pannetone, a rich, sweet bread originally from Milan, often shaped like a tall dome. One legend says that it got its name when an Italian baker named Tony wanted to impress his girlfriend's father. He created a rich bread studded with candied fruit and nuts so delicious that it persuaded the dubious father to allow Tony to marry his true love. In another version of the story, Tony was a lowly scullion in the kitchen of a grand household. When the head chef burned the Christmas cake, Tony improvised a sweet bread with the ingredients he had on hand. In all likelihood, the name comes from the Italian for "large loaf cake" or from the Milanese dialect for "luxury bread."

THE
BEGINNER'S
KITCHEN

A Baking Starter Kit: Essential Tools

If you've never baked before, you might wonder what equipment you'll need to get started. Surprisingly, you may have almost everything you need in your kitchen right now, but here's a helpful list.

Five-quart mixing bowl
You'll need bowls in other sizes in which to beat eggs or mix wet ingredients, but your mixing bowl should be large enough to hold two loaves' worth of dough, with high sides to keep the ingredients from escaping during mixing. Glass, glazed stoneware, Pyrex, or plastic will all do the job.

Accurate measuring cups and spoons
You'll need measuring cups for both dry and liquid ingredients, and yes, there is a difference—about 5% between the two. Consider spending a little more for the heavy-duty metal measuring cups and spoons—they're often on sale at Marshalls and T. J. Maxx. If you have recipes written in the European style, a scale will be essential.

A large wooden spoon
This is the hand tool of choice for most Breadheads, and this is another utensil you might want to spend a little more on—I've snapped eight or nine cheap wooden spoons in half over the years. There is also an unusual mixing tool that is specific to baking called a dough whisk that mixes and aerates batters and doughs better than any spoon in the drawer.

An instant-read thermometer

Get the electronic kind rather than one with a conventional dial, since they produce a precise temperature reading more quickly. You'll use it to test the temperature of liquids before adding yeast and to check the interior temperature of a loaf of bread to ensure that it is fully baked (see page 13 for details).

Baking pans

To start out, you'll need a baking sheet (like for cookies), loaf pans (I recommend the medium size, 8½" x 4½" x 2½"), and a 12-cup muffin tin. If you intend to make cinnamon rolls, a rolling pin and a 9" x 13" pan would be in order as well. As you explore the world of baking, you may start thinking about brioche pans, cast-iron skillets for scones, and stoneware casserole dishes for deep-dish pizza. But the aforementioned three or four pans will be adequate for most recipes. See page 128 for more information on how to choose the right pan for your recipe.

Wire racks

You can cool your loaves on a clean dish towel, but a wire rack allows for air circulation on the bottom of the loaf, resulting in a superior crust.

UTENSILS

Get the Right Knife and Keep It Sharp

The best bread knives have a wavy or scalloped edge rather than a serrated one. The points on a serrated knife can tear the crust. Keeping knives really sharp is a must—a dull knife is more likely to slip. Many people get their kitchen knives professionally sharpened at least once a year—some high-volume restaurants have them tended to every two weeks! At the very least, get a handheld sharpener and a steel and learn to use them. If you don't have a really sharp knife, chop parsley and other fresh herbs by placing the leaves in a coffee mug and using scissors to cut them to the desired size. If you have to cut up vegetables extra fine, use a pizza cutter.

Clean and Condition Your Cutting Boards

To remove strong scents from a wooden cutting board, sprinkle it with coarse salt and use a half a lemon as a scrubber. Rinse with water and dry thoroughly. The same method may be used to polish the copper bottom of a frying pan. Once a month, apply a small amount of food-grade mineral oil to wooden utensils and cutting boards to keep them well conditioned for years of use. If the surface of a wooden cutting board or butcher block becomes uneven after many years of use, it should either be planed smooth or replaced.

Which Pastry Blender to Use

You've probably seen recipes that call for you to cut shortening or butter into flour for biscuits or pastries. The tool you want is a pastry blender, but there are several versions of that tool. A wire pastry blender is perfect for soft fats like lard, shortening, or softened butter. A hard bladed pastry blender can do all those things plus it works for cold butter, like you need for puff pastry and scones. If you are working with soft fats, you can also go old school and use a "granny fork," which you can use to cut in shortening and mix the dough, like for old-fashioned cathead biscuits. But my blender of choice is the one with the hard blades.

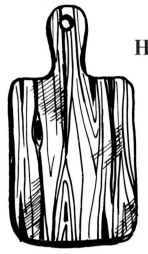

How to Choose (and Use) Cutting Boards

Contrary to popular belief, plastic cutting boards may not be safer than old-fashioned wooden ones. According to recent scientific research, bacteria on wooden cutting boards tend to sink below the surface, where they eventually die. Plastic cutting boards develop deeper grooves that are harder to clean out. The FDA's official position is that both are safe if they are cleaned well and replaced when they become deeply scarred. It's best to have two different cutting boards: one for meat and the other for vegetables, in order to prevent cross contamination. Use distinct sizes, shapes, or colors of boards to tell them apart.

Best Practices for Measuring Ingredients

- There is about a 5% difference in volume between dry and liquid measuring cups—use the right cup for your ingredients to ensure consistent results.
- Don't pour salt into a measuring spoon held over the mixing bowl—you can easily over pour and spoil your recipe. Keep salt in a wide-mouthed jar with a lid or some other airtight container that is large enough to allow you to scoop with a measuring spoon.
- To determine if a loaf of bread is done, use a digital instant-read thermometer. A fully baked loaf of white bread has an interior temperature of 190°F to 195°F. A denser multigrain bread like honey oatmeal may need to be baked to about 200°F.
- An empty squeeze bottle can be used to dispense batter evenly into mini muffin pans.

EGGS

How to Separate Egg Yolks from Whites

Many recipes call for you to separate the egg yolks from the whites. Waffles, for example, are lighter and fluffier if you add the yolks to the other liquid ingredients, but whisk the whites to the stiff peak stage and fold them into the batter. There are a number of handy gadgets to assist with this task, but if what if you are gadget-deprived? Separate egg yolks from the whites by placing a slotted spoon over a bowl and gently cracking the egg into the bowl of the spoon. The white will drop through, leaving the yolk in the bowl of the spoon. You can also crack the egg into a saucer, then gently squeeze an empty water bottle and use it to suck up the yolk.

How to Measure Egg Substitutes

Low-calorie egg substitute (the kind that comes in a carton) can be used in many recipes, and you can occasionally find cartons of homogenized and pasteurized whole eggs in the grocery store. But how to measure? A large egg adds about 3½ tablespoons of liquid to a recipe. This rule of thumb is also useful when substituting eggs of different sizes, for example, if you are collecting eggs from your own backyard chickens or receiving them from a neighboring farmer.

Try This Test to Determine Egg Freshness

Not sure just how long those eggs have been in the fridge? You can tell how fresh an egg is by submersing it in a bowl of cold water. If it's really fresh, it will lie on its side on the bottom. If it sinks but stands on end, it's less fresh and should be used soon. Eggs that float should be thrown out.

Dip Your Fingers to Snare Eggshell Fragments

Most of us have had this experience: you're cracking eggs to make an omelet and you see a little piece of eggshell in the bowl. You put a finger into the bowl to try to trap it against the side of the bowl, and it's like the shell is magnetized, repelled by your fingers and impossible to grasp. The solution is simple: dip your fingers in water first, and you'll be able to grab the fragment easily.

Use Eggs at Room Temperature

Eggs used for bread should be at room temperature when added to the mixture. Eggs add richness to the dough, which can slow down the rising process, and eggs straight from the fridge will cool down the dough and retard the rising process even more. If you can plan ahead, take eggs out of the fridge about 30 minutes before you are going to use them. Cold eggs can be placed in a bowl of hot tap water to warm them. If the recipe doesn't specify, then cold eggs will not affect the recipe.

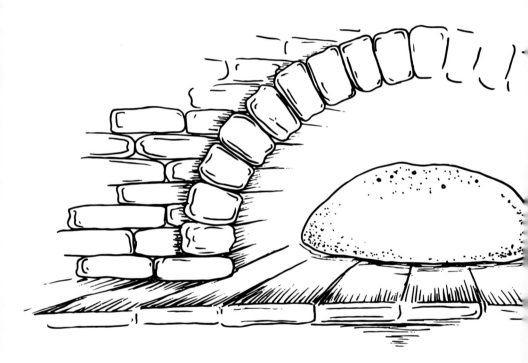

~

GLAZES, ICING, & FROSTING

~

Flavor Your Frostings with Dairy Creamers

There's not much my fellow monks like better for breakfast than homemade cinnamon rolls with a light drizzle of frosting. Most frosting or icing recipes include some vanilla extract for flavor. But you can achieve the same effect by using flavored half-and-half coffee creamers in place of the milk. Imagine cinnamon rolls or coffee cake with frosting flavored like French vanilla, Irish cream, hazelnut, or pumpkin spice! You can also add flavored half-and-half to beaten eggs to make gourmet French toast or bread pudding.

Introduce Steam for a Crispy Crust

Once people get into baking, they often want to create a loaf with a light, crispy crust like the baguettes in their favorite artisan bakery. First off, start with a simple recipe: water, yeast, flour, and salt. Dough with butter, eggs, and milk will make a rich dinner roll, but not a crusty loaf. You'll want to create steam in the oven in one of two easy ways. You can put a pan of hot water in the bottom of the oven (¾ cup is about right) or spray a mist of water over loaves just before they go into the oven. These methods keep the top of the dough moist so it rises higher and help form a thin outer layer of starch to produce a crisper crust. Baking on a pizza stone or other baking stone will also help the bottom crust stay crusty.

Make Your Crust Golden with Egg Wash

If you want to create an Instagram-worthy crust on a loaf of bread, use an egg wash. Just before putting a loaf of bread in the oven, use a soft pastry brush to coat it with egg white to make a crisper crust with a matte finish. Using an egg yolk beaten with a tablespoon of water will produce a rich, golden brown crust with a glossy shine. An even darker crust can be achieved by using an egg yolk mixed with milk. The proteins in the egg and the milk both contribute to browning.

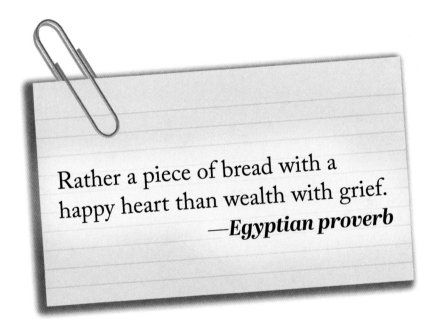

Rather a piece of bread with a happy heart than wealth with grief.
—*Egyptian proverb*

Frost with Corn Syrup for Optimal Sweetness

Many Danish pastries and other breakfast breads have a sweet filling, and a layer of frosting can sometimes overwhelm them. I find this to be especially true of the almond filling used in bear claws. For a light glaze on pastries that is just sweet enough, warm corn syrup for 10 seconds in the microwave, and brush it on with a soft pastry brush just before serving. Don't do this too far in advance or the corn syrup will be absorbed by the bread and make for a soggy crust.

How to Garnish with Seeds

Seeds like sesame, poppy, and sunflower can make a beautiful garnish for breads, especially braided loaves like challah or tsoureki. Brush the top of a risen loaf with milk before sprinkling on sesame or poppy seeds so they will stay in place during baking. Remember to use untoasted seeds for this purpose—the toasted ones will burn on the surface of the bread and should be used for salad or stir-fry instead.

NUTS

The Best Way to Store Nuts

Nuts are delicious in part because of their high oil content, but the oils in nuts can go rancid if not used promptly. They also tend to absorb flavors from other foods or the environment around them. Rather than store them in a cabinet or on a pantry shelf, keep nuts in an opaque, airtight container in the fridge or freezer. Minimizing exposure to heat and light will help keep them fresh longer, and using an airtight container will ensure that they keep their crunch.

Shop the Whole Store When Buying Nuts

Shop around within the entire supermarket when you are buying nuts. There can be a significant price difference in the products in the snack nut section (where they are more expensive), compared to the nuts in the baking aisle and in the produce section, which could be even less expensive. Whole nuts and large pieces stay fresh longer than the little packages of pre-chopped nuts, so buy whole or large pieces and chop them yourself. This also gives you more control over the size of the pieces. You might want larger nuggets for a banana bread but smaller ones to decorate the top of a coffee cake.

Benefits and Techniques of Toasting Nuts

Toasted nuts have more flavor and better crunch, especially desirable traits when they are used in batter breads or as garnishes for coffee cakes and pastries. When possible, you'll want to toast nuts whole, before they are chopped into smaller pieces. Preheat the oven to 325°F. Spread the nuts in a single layer on a rimmed baking sheet and bake for 10 to 20 minutes, depending on the size and type of the nuts. Stir them frequently during toasting to avoid burned spots. And set a timer! Nuts can burn in a very short time, and there's nothing more frustrating than wasting $10 worth of whole pecans because you got distracted by a phone call! It also helps to keep a raw nut out of the oven so you can use it to determine how dark the nuts are getting.

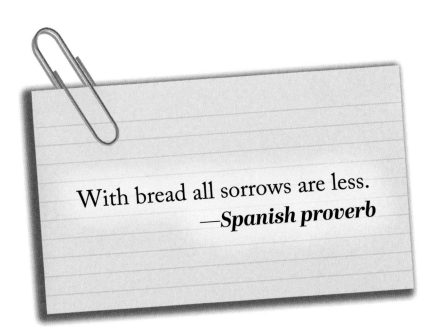

With bread all sorrows are less.
—*Spanish proverb*

OILS, FATS, & COOKING SPRAYS

Pick the Right Cooking Spray

The first aerosol pan release product, or cooking spray, became commonly available to the consumer in the 1960s. Since then, a greater variety has appeared, some of them with flavors added or with flour for coating pans for cakes and batter breads. Cooking spray can also be used to coat a measuring cup so that honey or molasses will slide out easily. Cheaper brands of cooking spray have a greater tendency to burn, especially when used in a hot skillet for pancakes or French toast, so buy the good stuff! When coating pans with cooking spray, place your pans in the sink or in your open dishwasher to avoid getting overspray on the counter, or worse yet, turning your kitchen floor into an oil slick!

Which Oils to Use and When

Oils, butters, and fats all behave differently and produce different flavors and effects. For example, using softened butter instead of melted will produce a more tender crumb in dinner rolls and loaf breads. Vegetable oil is preferable for sweet breads, and olive oil is best for savory recipes. (See page 121 for more details on the various kinds of olive oils.) Using shortening in a cornbread recipe will yield better flavor but more calories—you have been warned! Adding the oil to a yeasted bread dough after three quarters of the flour is incorporated will result in a lighter loaf. To produce tender pancakes with a crisp outer edge, fry them in butter. Never use diet spreads as a substitute for butter or regular margarine in a recipe. They have a high water content, and the added gums and starches add nothing in the way of flavor or texture.

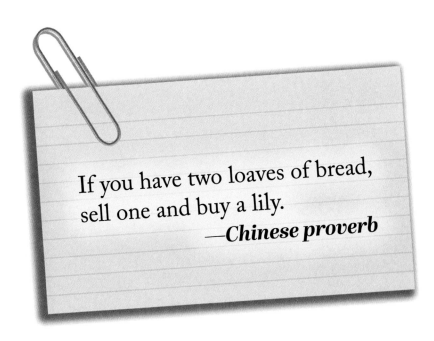

If you have two loaves of bread,
sell one and buy a lily.

—*Chinese proverb*

Yeast & Other Leaveners

When Buying Yeast, Check the Expiration Date

Dry yeast is available in individual packages, in strips of three packages, in jars, and in larger bags of one or two pounds. If you do a lot of baking, buy yeast in bulk and keep it in the refrigerator. You can buy a one-pound bag of yeast for less than $5 at many discount warehouse stores. Whether you buy in bulk or in smaller amounts, always check the expiration date before purchasing discounted dry yeast—it may be on sale because it is close to being no longer usable. Dry yeast remains viable for about two years after it is packaged.

Ways to Speed Up Yeast Activation

Traditional German bakers had a saying: "A pinch of ginger speeds the yeast"—and it's true! Adding ⅛ teaspoon of dried ginger to your initial mixture of yeast and liquid will help the yeast activate faster. Food scientists have discovered that cinnamon has a similar effect. A small amount of sugar is often added to the initial "proof" of the yeast as well.

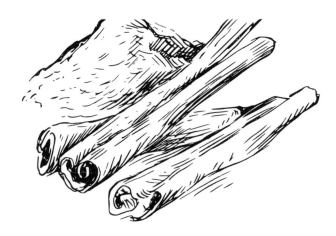

Did Fermented Beer or Yeast Breads Come First?

There is some debate over which came first: fermented beer or yeast breads—both use many of the same ingredients. In fact, the Latin name for the yeast we use for baking today—*Saccharomyces cerevisiae*—translates as "sugar-eating fungus for beer" (see page 3 for a little monastic history on the subject). The ancient Egyptians are thought to be the first culture to have developed yeasted breads, perhaps as early as 4000 BC, but the origins of brewing can be traced to roughly the same time.

Are Active Dry and Fast-Rising Yeasts Interchangeable?

If a recipe calls for active dry yeast and you have only fast-rising yeast on hand, you can still make the recipe without alteration. The reverse, however, is not true—recipes specifically calling for fast-rising yeast or instant yeast usually have mixing methods that won't work as well with active dry yeast. Many bakers keep both varieties in the pantry just in case.

What Makes a Yeast "Wild"?

The wild yeast used for sourdough varies from region to region because of the accompanying bacteria from the local environment. These lactobacilli produce different amounts of lactic acid and other additional flavors as the sourdough starter develops. That's why San Francisco sourdough has a sharper, tangier flavor than some sourdough breads made elsewhere, and it accounts for how some starters raise the dough more quickly than others. There are websites where you can obtain fresh sourdough starters from all over the world.

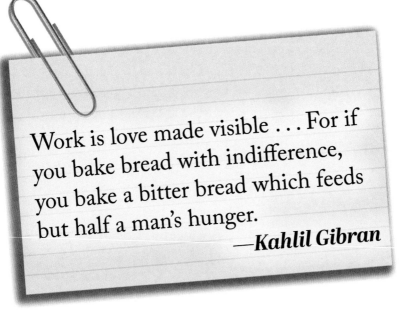

Work is love made visible ... For if you bake bread with indifference, you bake a bitter bread which feeds but half a man's hunger.
—*Kahlil Gibran*

What to Do if an Older Recipe Calls for Cake Yeast

In the early 1900s, cake yeast was delivered door to door by horse-drawn carts equipped with iceboxes. You may run across an old bread recipe that calls for "fresh" or "cake" yeast, which is not readily available in most supermarkets today. Adapt the recipe by using one package of active dry yeast for every four cups of flour in the recipe. A single package generally contains 2¼ teaspoons (7 grams) of active dry yeast. For those who use bulk yeast, there are spoons available that measure out the exact amount of yeast in a package.

When to Use Baking Soda vs. Baking Powder

Baking soda and baking powder are both used for quick breads like muffins, waffles, and cornbread, but they shouldn't be used interchangeably. Baking soda is used in recipes that have some sort of acidic liquid like buttermilk—think buttermilk biscuits and pancakes—while baking powder is activated by heat. Baking powder has a shelf life of about 9–12 months. If you are unsure if your supply is still usable, stir about half a teaspoon of baking powder into a cup of  hot water. If it's still usable, it will immediately start to fizz and bubble. Baking soda lasts considerably longer, but it can lose its effectiveness over time. To test it, add half a teaspoon of vinegar or lemon juice to a cup of warm water. Stir in half a teaspoon of baking soda—if it produces a lot of bubbles, it's still good.

OVENS & PANS

How to Find "Hot Spots" in Your Oven

Every oven has its own character, and some older models can be downright temperamental! So it's a good idea to have a professional recalibrate your oven's thermostat every few years to ensure accurate temperatures. If you suspect your oven has hot spots, check by spreading slices of bread in a single layer on baking sheets and placing them in a preheated 350°F oven for 15 to 20 minutes. Repeat this process with fresh slices on each shelf of the oven. You'll be able to tell which areas of the oven are hotter by the color of the bread.

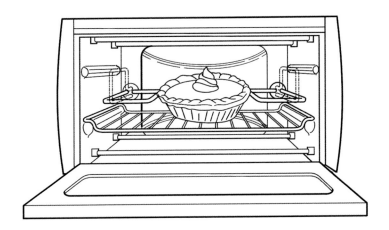

Don't Open the Oven While Baking

Opening the oven, even for a few seconds, can decrease the interior temperature by as much as 150°F. The sudden drop in temperature can even make some breads deflate, never to rise again. If possible, look through the oven window instead. If your bread seems to be browning too quickly in the oven, cover it lightly with a sheet of aluminum foil and consider a lower baking temperature next time. Breads with more sugar or eggs in the recipe will brown more quickly.

Know Your Pans and How They Differ

If you have less expensive baking sheets made of thin metal, double them up to keep the bottom of your baked goods from getting scorched. Dark-colored sheet pans will make the bottom of your loaves brown faster than those made of lighter metal; a darker interior of a loaf pan yields browner sides on your bread as well. See page 172 for more information on how the color of your pans can affect your baking. If your cookie sheets are stained with rust or grimy with baked-on grease, you can restore them. Put about ¼ cup of baking soda in a small bowl and add hydrogen peroxide to form a paste. Apply with a small sponge to rub out the stains.

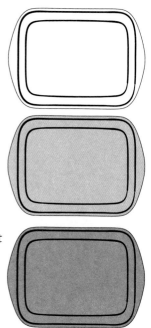

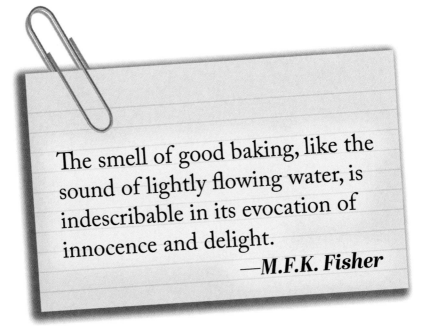

The smell of good baking, like the sound of lightly flowing water, is indescribable in its evocation of innocence and delight.

—**M.F.K. Fisher**

Rolling Out & Shaping Dough

How to Take Care of Your Rolling Pin

Never put a wooden or marble rolling pin into the dishwasher or soak it in the sink. Wipe them clean with a cloth dampened with warm water and dry promptly. Wooden rolling pins and other utensils will last longer if they receive a little TLC once a month or so. Rub them all over with a little food-safe mineral oil—just use your hands—and let it soak in for about 15 minutes. Then remove the excess with a clean, dry cloth. Can't find the rolling pin? Use a wine bottle instead!

Let the Dough Relax Before Rolling

Have you ever had the experience of making pizza dough and when you go to roll it out it keeps springing back into its original size? This elasticity is caused by the gluten strands in the dough, which were relaxed at the end of the rising process but tighten up again when the dough is punched down and kneaded. Instead of punching down, deflate the dough gently, divide, and shape it into slightly flattened balls, then let it rest for 10 to 15 minutes. This gives the gluten strands an opportunity to relax, making it easier to roll out. The same is true for the dough used for cinnamon rolls or donuts.

Using Leftover Biscuit Dough

Every time I make cut out biscuits, I have some dough scraps leftover, and if I squish the scraps together, the resulting biscuits never look right: they have weird shapes, they rise lopsided, etc. Many bakers just roll pieces of the dough in cinnamon sugar and bake a little snack. But here's a way to get two breads out of the same baking session. Cut or pull the scraps apart into small pieces. Put a tablespoon of melted butter, a tablespoon of honey, and a sprinkling of nuts into the cups of a muffin tin prepared with pan spray. Divide the dough scraps into the cups, (you might get only three or four muffins worth) then bake at 375 for 8 to 10 minutes. Now you have biscuits and mini monkey bread sticky buns!

Use the Right Cutters for Biscuits and Yeast Dough

You will sometimes see recipes that call for biscuits to be cut out with a drinking glass or Mason jar lid. However, their rounded edges can seal the sides of the biscuit and keep it from rising. Use a regular biscuit cutter instead, and try to avoid twisting the cutter too much. Your biscuits will rise higher and most evenly. If you need to cut yeast dough into strips (e.g., for butter fantans or Danish pastries), use a pizza cutter—it's easier to use than even the sharpest kitchen knife.

How to Smooth Loaf Tops

Beginning bakers are sometimes frustrated because their finished loaves are bumpy or uneven on the top. You give your loaves a smooth, professional look by grasping the sides of a portion of dough and tucking the ends underneath. Give the dough a quarter turn and repeat. Then roll the dough gently on the countertop to make it slightly elongated, and give it one last pull on the longer sides. The smooth top will not only be more attractive but will also better capture the carbon dioxide produced by the yeast and result in a loftier loaf.

HE SCORES

Techniques for Slashing and Scoring

One of the loveliest sights in the culinary world is a shelf piled with crusty French baguettes and dark, rustic loaves, each with a distinctive pattern scored on the top. The purpose of scoring, however, is not merely decorative. Slashing the top of the dough with a razor blade or a sharp knife allows it to expand during baking, especially in the first few minutes of baking. This initial expansion (called "oven spring") can result in unattractive cracks in the sides of a loaf. Slashing the loaves helps to control the direction in which the bread will expand.

First off, it can't be done with a dull blade. Without a sharp edge, your knife will drag and tear at the dough. The knife is supposed to do the work, without the baker having to press too hard. There is a specialized tool called a *lame* (pronounced "lahm") used by many professional bakers, but any really sharp knife will do the trick. I have a wicked sharp scalloped bread knife that works wonders, but don't even try with anything serrated—the points get caught and distort the top of the loaf.

Scoring bread is not for the timid—you have to work quickly and confidently. Some people like to wet or oil the blade when working with a wetter or stickier dough. The knife blade is held at an angle of 30 to 45 degrees to the surface of the loaf, and the cuts are made about ¼" deep. Some bakers score their loaves in decorative patterns—Pinterest is a good source of inspirational photos. Instructional videos also abound online, each with its distinctive technique and advice. Watch a few, but there's no substitute for regular practice.

Mixing, Kneading, & Rising

When (and How) to Mix Wet and Dry Ingredients

When you are mixing cake batter by hand (as opposed to with a stand mixer), the baker's rule of thumb is "wet into dry." The dry ingredients are whisked together in a bowl, and a "well," or depression, is formed in the center. Liquid ingredients are poured into the well, and flour is gradually pulled into the liquid until the batter is smooth. This method minimizes the development of gluten, which can make the cake tough. When mixing pancakes, waffles, and muffins, however, you can mix the dry ingredients into the wet because a few small lumps of flour won't hurt. Don't overbeat pancake or muffin batter, or they will turn out tough. A light stirring of 15 to 20 seconds is sufficient.

Develop a System for Prepping Ingredients

Before a restaurant line gets underway in the kitchen, the sous chef and other workers prepare the mise en place, from the French for "put in place." All the ingredients that will be needed to create that day's menu are prepared—everything from chopped parsley to chicken breasts—and are placed in the coolers or in containers along the back of the line or workspace. That way, food can be prepared as efficiently as possible, and substitutions can be planned for ingredients that are missing or apt to run out. The same system works well in a home kitchen too. Before beginning a recipe and getting underway, read the directions (twice). Make sure you have all the ingredients at hand, and if you are really ambitious, measure out the exact amounts into small bowls or ramekins on the counter. This preparation can save you a lot of time and frustration.

Create the Right Conditions for the Rising Process

All yeast bread recipes include at least one
or two periods of rising, sometimes more. In most
traditional home recipes, after the dough is mixed, it is placed in a clean
bowl, often with a light coating of oil to keep the top from drying out.
The bowl is covered with a clean, dry cloth and the dough left to rise for
at least an hour. The optimal temperature for this process of fermentation
is 75°F to 90°F. Loaves that are placed in a cooler location (65°F to
70°F) will take longer to rise but will produce superior flavor in the final
product. A dough enriched with butter, eggs, and/or sugar will take longer
to rise, and sourdough may require several hours of rising time. This
first rising is called the *ferment* because the yeast causes fermentation by
consuming the sugars and starches in the dough and producing alcohol
and carbon dioxide. The dough is then shaped and given a second rise
called the *proof* before going into the oven.

Knowing When Dough is Finished Rising

One of the things an experienced Breadhead learns is how to determine
if yeast dough has finished rising. There are three ways to tell that a
dough has completed its first rise, or ferment. The first is by time: most
recipes will tell you how long to allow the dough to ferment, usually 60 to
90 minutes. You can also tell that the dough is ready to be shaped if it has
doubled in bulk. The third method is to push a finger into the middle of
the dough. If the hole stays open, it's ready to be punched down, kneaded
and shaped. If it starts to close up, it needs more time. For the proofing
stage, loaves are ready to go in the oven when you push a finger gently
into the side of the dough and the dent springs back slightly.

The Science Behind Kneading

The purpose of kneading is twofold: to develop the gluten and to incorporate air into the dough. Two proteins in wheat flour, glutenin and gliadin, combine with water to form gluten, a stretchy protein molecule that wraps around itself during the process of kneading and forms a kind of net or matrix to capture the carbon dioxide produced by the fermentation of the yeast. The protein's stretchy quality is what allows the dough to rise and still keep its shape. The second purpose of kneading is also related to fermentation. According to Shirley Corriher in her fascinating book *BakeWise*, the carbon dioxide formed by the yeast does not form new bubbles but only flows into the air pockets already present in the dough. More air means more air pockets and hence a lighter loaf. To avoid adding too much flour while kneading by hand, dust your hands with flour instead of the countertop. This will keep the dough manageable without making it too dry.

How to Knead Wheat

Do you have a problem with your homemade whole wheat bread being dry or crumbly, or just too dense? There are a variety of solutions. You can add some nonfat dry milk powder to your recipe, or a cup of mashed potatoes. But most likely the problem is that you are adding too much flour during the kneading process. Whole wheat flour and other whole grains like oatmeal or cornmeal absorb the liquid from your recipe more slowly than the finer particles of all-purpose flour. So you can be fooled into adding too much flour while kneading. Don't put in that last half cup of flour. Leave the dough a little sticky at first, knead for four minutes, and then let it rest for 20 minutes. You'll find that it has firmed up considerably and you will not need to add much more flour during the last 4 or 5 minutes of kneading.

THE
UNKINDEST CUT

Important Knife Safety Tips

One of the most common forms of kitchen accidents is cutting oneself with a knife, especially a dull one. Cutting raw chicken is the number one culprit, with potatoes, apples, and onions not far behind. As far as bread is concerned, slicing one's palm while cutting a bagel in half is the kitchen laceration that most often sends careless people to the ER.

Some knife safety tips:
- Keep your knives sharp—a dull knife requires more pressure and is more likely to slip and cut you.
- Do not hold food in your hand—especially bagels!—while you cut.
- Keep knife handles clean and dry during food preparation—a wet or greasy knife is dangerous to use.
- Use a cutting board and place a damp towel underneath it to keep it stable on the countertop.
- Do not slice or chop anything while distracted—keep your eyes on the blade.
- Do not leave a knife hidden in a sink of soapy water—you can easily reach in and get a bad cut.
- Wash knives by hand immediately after use, keeping the sharp edge of the blade away from you while washing and drying.
- A knife block is a safer way to store knives than in a drawer.

SUBSTITUTIONS

Making Dairy Substitutions

- Why buy a quart of buttermilk when you only need a cup for biscuits? Just add 1 tablespoon of vinegar or lemon juice to a scant cup of 2% or skim milk. Let stand for 10 minutes before using. A quarter cup of sour cream added to ¾ cup of skim milk will also serve.
- There's no substitute for heavy cream if whipped cream is your goal, but if you need cream as a baking ingredient or for a sauce, you can use two parts whole milk to one part melted butter (unsalted).
- Full-fat Greek yogurt can be a substitute for sour cream in coffee cakes and batter breads.
- Run cottage cheese through a food processor until smooth to make a quick substitute for ricotta cheese.

Substituting Spices

- Equal parts of cinnamon and ground cloves make an easy substitute for the less commonly used allspice.
- A small clove of garlic is the equivalent of ⅛ teaspoon of garlic powder.
- If a recipe calls for dried herbs and you are using fresh, double the amounts, except for rosemary and sage. These strong herbs should be used in the same amounts, fresh or dry.
- If you need a teaspoon of pumpkin pie spice, make your own with ½ teaspoon cinnamon, ¼ teaspoon ginger, ⅛ teaspoon nutmeg, and ⅛ teaspoon cloves.

Substitutions in Batter Breads

- Don't care for the slightly metallic taste of some baking powders? Make your own with 1 teaspoon of baking soda, 2 teaspoons of cream of tartar, and 1 teaspoon of cornstarch.
- Yellow bananas can be speed ripened for banana bread by roasting them in a preheated 300°F oven for 40 minutes. They'll have the perfect consistency for a soft, moist loaf.
- If you're making a batter bread and find yourself short by one egg, substitute 3 tablespoons of mayonnaise.
- If a recipe calls for a cup of self-rising flour, you can make your own with 1 cup of all-purpose flour, 1½ teaspoons of baking powder, and ¼ teaspoon of salt.
- Trying to make a healthier version of your favorite batter bread? Substitute applesauce for half of the oil or butter in the recipe.

How to Make a Pizza Crust in a Pinch

Homemade pizza is the best, but you may not always have time to wait for a yeasted dough to rise. A quick substitute is at hand! Place 1 cup of plain Greek yogurt with 1½ cups of self-rising flour in a stand mixer, and use a dough hook to mix it on medium for 6 minutes. Let rest for 10 minutes before rolling it out. Use a hot oven (500°F) to bake your pizza in order to get a crisp, browned crust. Using a preheated pizza stone will also prevent soggy crusts.

~

TROUBLESHOOTING

~

How to Speed Up a Slow Rise

If your bread is rising too slowly because the house is cold, place a pan of very hot water on the bottom shelf of the oven. Then place your pans on the middle shelf to rise. The warm, moist air will create the perfect environment for the yeast to develop. Just remember to take them out in time to preheat the oven! You can use the same method if your dough is rising slowly because the dough is enriched with sugar or eggs, like challah, or has a lot of butter, like brioche.

Possible Causes of Doorstop Bread

A heavy, dense loaf may be the result of any number of problems.

- Expired yeast is often the culprit. Check the expiration date on your yeast before starting the recipe.
- There may not be enough yeast in the recipe to make the dough rise. One package of yeast per 4 cups of flour is the usual proportion. Artisan breads use less yeast and longer rising periods, so follow those recipes exactly.
- Using liquids that are too hot can kill the yeast—use an instant-read thermometer to make sure your liquids are under 130°F. The ideal temperature for proofing yeast is 100°F, or about the temperature you might use for baby formula. Some fast-rising yeast breads require higher temperatures—follow the directions carefully for these recipes.
- Insufficient kneading could be the culprit. When kneading by hand, 6 to 8 minutes of kneading should develop the dough to the correct consistency.

Possible Causes of Crumbly Bread

Does your bread crumble and fall apart when you cut it? You may have added too much flour or used too high of a proportion of whole wheat flour. Under-kneaded dough may also have a crumbly texture. Large holes at the top of a cut loaf are an indication that the loaf is "over proofed"—it rose too long before being placed in the oven. Similarly, if a loaf deflates after it comes out of the oven, it may be over-risen or underbaked.

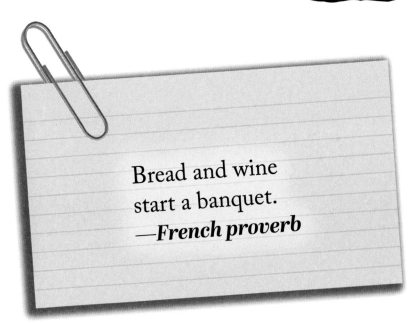

Bread and wine start a banquet.
—*French proverb*

ADD SOME WHOLE GRAINS

Add Whole Grains to Your Diet with This Easy Mix

"Whole grains are healthier!"
"Whole grains are good for you!"
"Whole grains have more fiber and more flavor!"

Whole grains are a pain in the rump.

Not really, but it's inconvenient to open up four or five different canisters every time you want to make healthier waffles. This whole grain mix is easy to make, keeps well, and can be substituted for some or all of the white flour in many quick bread recipes (like the baking mix on page 76). In the abbey kitchen, I keep a two-gallon tub of this particular blend on hand so I can easily add a little whole grain goodness at a moment's notice. This recipe makes a more modest amount, but keep it in the fridge if you don't bake often—the whole wheat can go rancid in the heat of the kitchen.

4 cups stone-ground whole grain wheat flour
1 cup yellow cornmeal
1 cup old-fashioned oats
⅓ cup flaxseed meal
Mix thoroughly and store in an airtight container.

BAKING MIX

An All-Purpose Mix with No-Nonesense Ingredients

And a Recipe for Cheddar Chive Biscuits to Boot

There's no question that boxed mixes are convenient aids to baking, but the amount of salt, sugar, partially hydrogenated oils, and preservatives can be troubling. This homemade baking mix can be used for biscuits, pancakes, and muffins, and you can control the ingredients based on your dietary needs. Want more fiber? Use half whole wheat flour. Need to reduce processed sugar or salt in your diet? Adjust the recipe accordingly.

6 cups all-purpose flour
3 tablespoons baking powder
3 tablespoons granulated sugar
1 tablespoon salt
2 sticks unsalted butter, cubed

Place flour, baking powder, sugar, and salt in a food processor, and process until mixed and fluffy. Add butter and pulse until evenly combined. Store in an airtight container in the refrigerator for up to three months.

Because the recipe uses butter instead of shortening, it must be refrigerated, but you'll find plenty of reasons to use it. It may seem like six cups is a large amount, but two cups are needed to make a dozen small biscuits—like these cheddar chive drop biscuits, which can be ready in about 15 minutes.

Cheddar Chive Drop Biscuits

2 cups baking mix
½ cup shredded cheddar cheese
2 tablespoons fresh minced chives
¾ cup 2% or skim milk

Place baking mix in a bowl, and stir in cheese and chives. Make a well in the center of the mixture, and pour in milk. Stir until just moistened. Drop by large tablespoons a couple of inches apart on a lightly oiled baking sheet. Bake in a preheated oven at 450°F for 8 to 10 minutes or until lightly browned. You can also brush the biscuits with a little garlic butter once they've cooled slightly. Makes 10 to 12 drop biscuits.

COBBLER

Cobblers, Crisps, Betty, and Buckle— Definitions

There are thousands of variations on desserts that make use of fresh fruit and some kind of dough or crust. Here's a primer on how to tell them apart.

Cobblers are baked in a pan or casserole dish, with sweetened fruit on the bottom and clumps of biscuit dough on the top. The surface of the dessert looks like an old-fashioned cobblestone street, hence the name. They are best with stone fruit like peaches and apricots but can also be made with berries. A **grunt** is like a cobbler but is cooked in a covered pan on a stove top—the name comes from the grunting noise the bubbling fruit makes.

Crisps also have sweetened fruit on the bottom, but they have a streusel topping made of butter, flour, sugar, and (often) oats—they may also have nuts in the topping. A **crumble** is similar to a crisp, but the topping is coarser in texture and always contains oats.

Apple crisp, however, should not be confused with **apple brown betty**, which has sweetened slices of apples alternating in layers with buttered crumbs. This thrifty colonial dessert was popular with pioneer homestead women because it could be cooked in a cast-iron pot over a hearth or open fire and could be made with over-ripe apples and stale bread.

Another colonial favorite was **apple pandowdy**, which starts with a layer of rolled-out pastry dough or pie crust, adds a layer of apple filling (often sweetened with molasses), and is topped with another layer of dough. About halfway through the baking process, the top crust is broken up with a knife or spoon and pushed down unevenly into the apple layer (the "dowdying" of the pan).

A **buckle** is a fruit-studded coffee cake with a streusel topping. It takes its name from the fact that the surface of the cake buckles unevenly during baking. The German version of this might be called a *kuchen*. Buckles are usually made with berries and are often enriched with sour cream.

I like reality;
it tastes like bread.
—*Jean Anouilh*

~

LITTLE
REWARDS

~

The Story Behind Pretzels—and a Recipe

You might think of pretzels as a crunchy part of your sack lunch or a stadium snack of soft dough covered in kosher salt or melted cheese. But according to legend, the pretzel started out as a treat for children who had memorized their prayers. A monk in Italy around 610 AD folded strips of dough into a shape resembling arms crossed in prayer. He called these treats "pretiolas," or "little rewards." Of course, there's no documented evidence to confirm this story, and similar stories are found in France and Germany.

Pretzels appear on the crest of a 12th-century German bakers' guild and in a manuscript illustration in a 15th-century prayer book. Pretzel street vendors in European cities and towns were common from the mid-1400s onward. By this time, pretzels were considered a sign of good luck—they were worn around the neck on New Year's Day, hung on Christmas trees, and even hidden on Easter for children to find. Pretzels were popular during Lent because they are made from a simple, unenriched dough and conformed to the penitential austerities of the season.

German immigrants brought the pretzel to America in the 1700s, especially to the Pennsylvania region, and even today around 80% of pretzels made in America are made in that state. Up until the mid-19th century, all pretzels were the soft variety; commercial bakeries started producing harder pretzels because they kept longer and could be shipped further away.

Hard pretzels are now one of the best-selling salty snacks in America, and soft pretzels continue to be popular food for pushcart pretzel vendors, mall food courts, and sports stadiums. But homemade pretzels are far better—here's a recipe:

Soft Pretzels

1½ cups warm water (110°F)
1 pkg. (2¼ teaspoons) active dry yeast
2 tablespoons barley malt syrup or
dark honey
4½ cups unbleached all-purpose flour
2 teaspoons salt
4 tablespoons unsalted butter, melted

2 quarts water
¼ cup baking soda
Pretzel salt, for sprinkling

In a medium-size bowl, combine the water, yeast, and malt syrup/honey, and then whisk. Let develop about 5 minutes, until frothy. Stir in salt and melted butter until combined. Add 4 cups of flour, one cup at a time, mixing thoroughly each time until incorporated. Turn out onto a lightly floured board, and knead for 5 to 8 minutes, adding more flour as needed to make a smooth and elastic dough that is only slightly sticky. Lightly oil the surface of the dough and place in a clean, dry bowl. Cover with a dry cloth, and let rise about an hour or until doubled. Punch the dough down, and knead it lightly.

Cut the dough in quarters, and then, cut each quarter in thirds, making 12 pieces. Roll each piece out into an 18" rope and shape into a pretzel. Place pretzels on a lightly greased baking sheet, and allow to rise for 15 minutes.

Preheat oven to 425°F. Pour the two quarts of water into a large skillet or pan and bring to a boil. Dissolve the baking soda in the water. Gently lower two or three pretzels into the water at a time, and allow them to boil 1 minute; turn pretzels over and boil for another minute. Gently remove pretzels from water with a pair of tongs or slotted spoon, and place on cloth towels to drain briefly—don't use terry cloth or you'll get fuzz! While the surface of the dough is still damp, place the pretzels on a well-greased baking sheet—a silicone baking mat is even better—and sprinkle each pretzel with pretzel salt (kosher salt will do in a pinch). Bake for 15 to 20 minutes. Cool slightly on wire racks and serve warm.

FOOD HOLIDAY MASH-UPS & RECIPES FOR ALL SEASONS

I've been researching food holidays, and based on what I could find online, there are an astonishing number of food-related "holidays" in the course of a calendar year, celebrating everything from dietary fiber to decadent desserts. It seems as though every fruit, vegetable, bread group, and protein has a special day. Which prompts one to ask: How are such days established?

The president of the United States, of course, has the authority to declare a commemorative event or day by proclamation—so can state legislatures and local mayors, for more regional celebrations. But in the end, like most things political, it's all about lobbying. Petitions are usually introduced by trade associations or public relations firms hired by the portion of the food industry responsible for a particular food's sale and distribution. 'Twas ever thus.

But let's not be too cynical about how the holidays got put on the calendar. I would be happy to enjoy cream puffs (January 2), oatmeal nut waffles (March 11), or falafels (June 12) on *any* day of the year without any inspiration beyond my own love for baked goods. So for the following section, I've selected some monthly food designations and mashed them up with a food "day" in that same period: National Dairy Month in June plus National Donut Day on the first Friday of that month equals a recipe for Sour Cream Donuts (see page 100). I'll include a little background on the holiday, and share a recipe so you can have a reason to celebrate too.

After all, I've been saying for years that people don't need recipes as much as they need *reasons* to bake. The reason could be ethnic heritage, holiday tradition, an abundant backyard garden, or a gorgeous picture on Pinterest—or National Homemade Bread Day (November 17). For this last, I intend to take the day off from teaching and head to the kitchen!

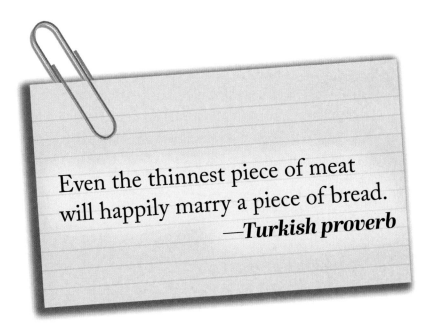

Even the thinnest piece of meat will happily marry a piece of bread.
—*Turkish proverb*

January

The first month of the year is National Fiber Focus Month—I am not making this up. I suspect nutritionists were hoping to hitch a ride on everyone's New Year's resolutions! Women should try to get at least 25 grams of fiber per day, while the recommended amount for men is 38 grams. Fruits, vegetables (especially beans), and nuts are good sources of fiber, along with whole grains. Whole wheat flour, old-fashioned oatmeal, and brown rice are examples of fiber-rich grains. See page 72 for a multigrain flour mix you can use in bread recipes to increase your fiber intake.

I'm all for adding more fiber to the diet, but there are some breakfast foods out there that have more fiber than baling twine and about as much flavor. I like to sneak fiber into my fellow monks' diet by adding whole grain flours to something like pancakes or waffles. Fortunately, January 28 is National Blueberry Pancake Day—a clear sign of Divine Providence. Blueberries are among those fruits that still taste good after being frozen and thawed, so you can enjoy them year-round. Don't blow your "eat healthier" New Year's resolution by making a boxed mix with "blueberry flavor bits"— you could have these whole grain delights made up in no time.

Whole Wheat Blueberry Pancakes

¾ cup whole wheat flour
½ cup all-purpose flour
1 tablespoon brown sugar or honey
1 teaspoon baking powder
½ teaspoon salt
¼ teaspoon baking soda
1 cup fat-free or 2% milk
2 tablespoons vegetable oil
1 egg
½ teaspoon vanilla extract
1 cup blueberries

In a medium-sized bowl, place flours, sugar, baking powder, salt, and baking soda, and whisk until well blended. Whisk together milk, oil, egg, and vanilla into a small bowl. Form a well in the center of the dry ingredients, pour wet mixture into the center of the well. Stir together until just combined. It's OK to have a few lumps remain—do not overmix. Gently fold in blueberries. If batter seems too thick, stir in 1 or 2 tablespoons of milk.

Prepare a large nonstick skillet or griddle with cooking spray, and heat over medium heat until hot. Form pancakes by pouring about ¼ cup of batter for each onto the pan. Cook about 1½ to 2 minutes or until large bubbles form on top and bottom is browned. Turn with a spatula and cook about 1 minute more. To serve, sprinkle with confectioners' sugar or drizzle lightly with syrup or honey. Makes 8 to 10 pancakes.

February

February's designation as National Hot Breakfast Month was not promoted by diners or pancake houses, but by educational advocates. Numerous studies show that kids who get a hot breakfast do better in school. Dozens of studies, some of them from as far back as the 1950s, have consistently shown that children who eat breakfast perform better academically than those who don't. And what they eat for breakfast matters too. Sugary cereals and pastries cause a spike in blood sugar levels followed by a crash two hours later, sometimes accompanied by changes in mood as well as a reduced ability to focus. Whole grain foods and protein help keep energy levels more stable.

The same is true for adults, so how about a hot breakfast bread that also brings the heat in spiciness? February 20 is National Muffin Day, so why not skip the toaster pastries and the fast-food drive-through and try a spicy sausage muffin? Make them the night before, and pop one in the microwave in the morning for a flavorful wake-up call. I like to slice mine in half and top it with a poached egg, but you could also crumble it up with your scrambled eggs.

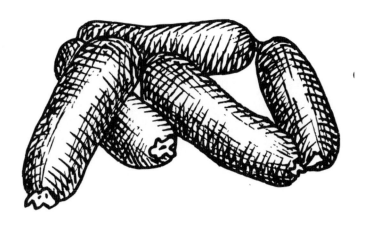

Hot Sausage Muffins

8 ounces bulk hot Italian sausage*
2 cups baking mix (see page 76)
½ teaspoon granulated garlic
⅛ teaspoon ground pepper
4 ounces pepper jack cheese, shredded
14-ounce can of pizza sauce
1 egg
2 tablespoons olive oil

Preheat oven to 400°F. Grease a 12-cup muffin tin or use paper liners (I recommend the former if you are serving them right away, the latter if you are making them the night before and reheating them the next morning).

Fry sausage in a skillet until cooked and browned, breaking the sausage up into small pieces as you cook it. Don't drain it—you'll use the sausage and the flavorful grease in the batter. Whisk together baking mix, garlic, and pepper in a medium-sized bowl. Pour pizza sauce into another bowl, and beat the egg and oil into it. Add sausage with its pan drippings and mix well. Pour the wet mixture into the dry ingredients, and mix just until not quite blended. Fold in the cheese. Scoop the batter into muffin cups (it will be quite thick). Bake 20 to 25 minutes or until firm on top. Cool 15 to 20 minutes before serving.

You can also buy links and remove sausage from the casings—two large sausages should be enough.

March

In my family, March is most notable for St. Patrick's Day, which in my Grandma Tootsie's mind had the status of a national holiday combined with a Catholic holy day of obligation. Had she known it was also National Flour Month, we would have celebrated that too. March 7 is National Cereal Day, being the anniversary of the accidental invention of corn flakes in 1894 by Dr. John Harvey Kellogg. My attempts to combine all three holidays into a corn-flake-infused Irish soda bread proved fruitless, so you'll have to make do with this delicious bread that also makes use of honey and oat flour.

Honey Oat Corn Flake Bread

1 cup crushed corn flakes

1 cup oat flour

2 cups hot water

⅓ cup honey

3 tablespoons butter

2 teaspoons salt

2 packages active dry yeast

4 to 4½ cups unbleached bread flour

In a large mixing bowl, combine crushed corn flakes, oat flour, water, honey, butter, and salt. Stir until thoroughly blended, and then cool the mixture to lukewarm. In a small bowl, proof the yeast in a quarter-cup of warm water. When corn flake mixture is lukewarm, add yeast; mix thoroughly and allow to develop for 10 minutes.

Add the bread flour, one cup at a time, mixing thoroughly after each cup, until you have a fairly stiff dough. Turn out onto a lightly floured board, and knead for 5 minutes. Cover and allow the dough to rest for 5 or 10 minutes. Then resume kneading for 5 to 7 minutes, incorporating more flour as needed. The dough will remain slightly sticky but should be quite elastic. Lightly coat the surface of the dough with butter, and place it back in the rinsed mixing bowl. Cover with a dish towel and let rise until doubled, 1 to 1½ hours. Punch dough down.

Form into loaves and place in greased pans. Let rise until nearly doubled, about 45 minutes. Bake at 375°F for about 35 to 45 minutes. Lightly cover the loaves with aluminum foil if the tops begin to brown too quickly. Loaves are done when they come out from the pan easily and sound hollow when tapped on the bottom. Cool on racks.

Notes
Place the corn flakes in a plastic bag and run over it with a rolling pin until the crumbs are in small pieces. The corn flakes tend to break up the gluten network that holds the dough together, so make sure you knead thoroughly. Otherwise, your dough won't have enough body to hold up during the rising and baking process, and the loaf will collapse as it cools.

April

April may be "the cruelest month," according to T. S. Eliot, but it has the best food holidays. Among my favorite foods fêted this month: peanut butter and jelly (the second), caramel popcorn (the sixth), coffee cake (the seventh), licorice (the 12th), animal crackers (the 18th), pigs-in-a-blanket (the 24th), and zucchini bread (the 25th). It's also Garlic Month, and that, combined with Beer Day on the seventh, should inspire you to make this Cheesy Garlic Beer Bread. It's an easy quick bread that mixes in minutes and makes the kitchen smell terrific.

Cheesy Garlic Beer Bread
2½ cups all-purpose flour
1 teaspoon salt
2½ teaspoons baking powder
2 tablespoons granulated sugar
1 (12-fluid ounce) can or bottle beer, room temperature
½ cup shredded smoked Cheddar cheese
¼ cup (½ stick) unsalted butter
½ teaspoon garlic powder

Preheat oven to 350°F, and lightly grease a 9" x 5" loaf pan. Melt butter and whisk in garlic powder—set aside. In a large bowl, stir together flour, salt, baking powder, and sugar. Gently stir in beer, then cheese. Spoon batter into prepared loaf pan and spread evenly. Pour garlic butter on top of loaf. Bake for 50 to 60 minutes, until a toothpick inserted into center of loaf comes out clean. Remove from pan, and cool on a wire rack. Makes 12 to 16 servings.

May

Many foods have both a day and a month dedicated to them. May is National Egg Month, but eggs are fêted on June 3 as well. May is National Strawberry Month, with National Pick Strawberries Day on the 20th, and National Biscuit Day on the 29th. I decided to mash all these together into Strawberry Biscuits, but my recipe uses an (untraditional) egg. Serve them with Honey Coriander Butter, because the first full week of May is National Herb Week.

Strawberry Biscuits with Honey Coriander Butter

3 cups all-purpose flour
1 tablespoon baking powder
1 tablespoon
½ teaspoon cream of tartar
½ teaspoon salt
¾ cup cold butter (1½ sticks) cut into pieces
1 egg
1 cup whole milk or half-and-half
1 cup chopped ripe strawberries

Preheat oven to 425°F. In a medium-sized bowl, combine flour, baking powder, sugar, cream of tartar, and salt; whisk until blended. Cut in butter with a pastry blender or two knives until the mixture resembles coarse crumbs. Beat egg and half-and-half together, and stir into flour mixture until just moistened. Add strawberries and stir until evenly distributed. Turn dough out onto a lightly floured surface, and knead gently about 30 seconds, just enough to bring the dough together.

Roll out to 1" thickness. Cut with a floured 2½" biscuit cutter. Push straight down, firmly, and do not twist the cutter—you'll get better loft on your biscuits that way. Push scraps together, and gently reroll to cut out more. Place rounds on a lightly greased baking sheet. Bake at 425°F for 12 to 15 minutes or until golden brown. Remove from pan and cool briefly on a wire rack before serving warm with Honey Coriander Butter. Makes about a dozen.

Honey Coriander Butter
1 stick unsalted butter
¼ cup honey
1 teaspoon ground coriander

Mix ingredients together in a small bowl. Better if made at least an hour ahead of time, but best if made the day before.

June

National Milk Month was established in 1937, but it soon evolved into a month celebrating all things dairy. The first Friday in June is National Donut Day, first promoted as a fundraiser in 1938 for The Salvation Army in Chicago and to honor The Salvation Army "Lassies" of World War I, who served donuts to soldiers. In World War II, female Red Cross volunteers were referred to as "Doughnut Dollies," and many veterans came home and used the small business loans provided by the GI Bill to open donut shops. Although cold milk goes well with just about any donut, these sour cream donuts are especially good dusted with powdered sugar and served with chocolate milk.

Sour Cream Donuts
3¾ cups all-purpose flour
⅓ cup sugar
1½ teaspoons baking powder
½ teaspoon salt
¼ teaspoon baking soda
1½ cups sour cream
1 egg
oil for frying (about 2½" to 3" deep)

Sift together dry ingredients into a medium-sized bowl. In a separate bowl, combine egg and sour cream. Pour liquid mixture into dry mixture, and stir until just moistened. Turn dough out onto a lightly floured surface, and knead about 8 strokes, just enough make a cohesive dough. As with biscuits, it really is crucial to handle the dough as little as possible, or else the donuts will be tough rather than light and tender. Let dough rest for 10 minutes.

On a lightly floured surface, roll dough out to a thickness of about ½", and cut out donuts using a 3" or 4" donut cutter. Press dough scraps together gently (do not knead), reroll and cut more donuts. Do not roll a third time—just fry the scraps as oddly shaped donut holes. Let donuts firm up, uncovered, for about 30 minutes—I usually cut mine out and then place them on a lightly greased cookie sheet. Preheat oil to 365°F–375°F. (I recommend using an electric fryer with a calibrated dial, but you can use a deep skillet on the stovetop if you have a candy thermometer.) Fry donuts three or four at a time, about 2 minutes per side, until medium brown. Drain on paper towels. Sprinkle with powdered sugar on one side, and serve warm with ice-cold chocolate milk. Makes 20 to 24 of the 3" donuts plus donut holes.

July

July is designated National Culinary Arts Month, with a grateful nod to all culinary professionals, from TV celebrity chefs to the underappreciated line cook who makes the best hash browns at the local diner. Culinary training runs the gamut from small classes at cooking stores to junior college degree programs to Le Cordon Bleu. But the term "culinary arts" always reminds me of the sign above the doorway to a barn-like structure at the Peoria Heart of Illinois Fair, where my mother entered her bread every year (her raisin bread took first place nearly every time she entered it).

I love fair food in general and fried foods in particular: corn dogs, haystack onion rings, and funnel cakes are my personal faves. But there was one year at the Heart of Illinois Fair when a local church set up a tiny trailer out of which they sold fresh corn fritters. These fried delights were dredged in powdered sugar and served piping hot in a brown lunch paper bag. I devoured several bags' worth over the course of the week of the fair and eagerly anticipated their return the following year. But alas, I was disappointed in my expectation—the little trailer with the hand-printed cardboard sign never returned. You'll have to settle for the homemade version yourself and hope they are as good as my memories.

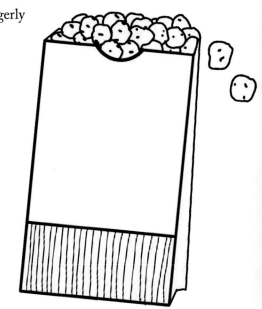

Corn Fritters

Oil for frying
1 cup all-purpose flour
2 teaspoons sugar
1 teaspoon baking powder
¼ teaspoon salt
2 large eggs
½ cup milk
2 teaspoons vegetable oil
1 12-ounce can of corn,
drained (¾ cup, fresh)
Powdered sugar for coating

Heat at least 2" of oil to 375°F, either in an electric fryer or in a heavy pan over medium heat. You may use an electric deep fryer as well. Measure flour, sugar, baking powder, and salt into a bowl, and whisk to combine ingredients thoroughly. In a separate bowl, beat eggs, milk, and oil together, and then stir in the corn kernels. Pour wet mixture into the bowl with the dry ingredients, and stir until thoroughly combined. Drop tablespoons of the batter into the hot oil and fry until golden brown on both sides—they may need some help turning over. It takes only 2 or 3 minutes for them to cook, so don't crowd the pan or the oil will cool and the fritters will be soggy with grease. Remove the fritters to drain on a paper towel, and then roll them while warm in the powdered sugar to coat (some people prefer granulated sugar). Serve immediately.

August

I don't know why August is National Sandwich Month, by which I mean I don't know why someone chose August, nor why we need a month to promote sandwiches in the first place. I don't know too many people who don't eat sandwiches, and when fast-food joints started serving food *other* than sandwiches, *that* was a reason to celebrate. But you might consider going beyond burgers and subs this month and try a Mexian *cemita*, a muffuletta from New Orleans, or a banh mi sandwich.

Or better yet, on August 15, celebrate the birthday of the icon of French cooking, Julia Child, by making this Cordon Bleu Grilled Cheese Sandwich, with the flavor profile of the famous chicken dish named after the cooking school in Paris where she trained.

Cordon Bleu Grilled Cheese Sandwich

2 teaspoons sour cream
½ teaspoon Dijon mustard
1½ teaspoons olive oil
2 slices hearty country bread
2 thin slices Swiss cheese
1 slice deli ham
1 thick slice chicken breast

Mix sour cream and Dijon mustard in a small dish and set aside. Over medium heat, heat oil in a skillet. Layer ingredients as follows: 1 slice of bread, 1 slice of cheese, ham, chicken, and the second slice of cheese. Spread sour cream mixture over second slice of bread and place on top, sour cream side down. Cook 3 minutes or until bread is browned and crisp. Turn over and cook 2 more minutes, and then remove pan from heat and cover. When sandwich is warmed through and cheese is melted, transfer the sandwich to a cutting board and cut in half to serve.

September

Every year in September, we harvest the honey from the monastery's hives, always a cause for rejoicing among my monastic brethren—we keep a small pitcher of honey on every table in the dining room. So in honor of September's position as both National Honey Month and Whole Grains Month, with National Raisin Day on the 30th, I'm sharing a recipe for Raisin Walnut Bread that uses stone-ground rye flour in the dough and honey as the sweetener.

Raisin Walnut Bread

1 cup lukewarm milk

1 cup lukewarm water

2 tablespoons dark honey

2 packages active dry yeast

2 cups stone-ground rye flour, divided

2 tablespoons vegetable oil

1½ teaspoons salt

3 to 3½ cups bread flour

2 cups raisins

1 cup walnuts, chopped

In a large bowl, mix milk, water, honey, yeast, and one cup of rye flour. Allow yeast to develop for 5 minutes. Then add oil and salt; mix well. Stir in the remainder of the rye flour, and allow dough to rest for 10 minutes as the rye flour absorbs moisture. Add 3 cups of the bread flour, one cup at a time, mixing thoroughly each time. Turn dough out onto a lightly floured board, and knead vigorously for 8 to 10 minutes, adding enough of the remaining bread flour to make a firm (but not stiff) dough that is slightly sticky.

Rinse out the bowl. Lightly oil the surface of the dough, and place it back in the bowl; cover with a towel. Allow to rise in a warm area free from drafts for 60 to 75 minutes, or until doubled in bulk. Punch down dough and knead briefly to work out the larger air bubbles. Roll the dough out to a thickness of about ½". Sprinkle nuts and raisins on top of the dough. Fold the edges of the dough toward the center, and knead for a few strokes to distribute the raisins and nuts evenly. (At first it will be messy and seem to be falling apart, but be patient; it will all come together.)

Divide the dough in two, and shape into loaves. Place loaves in lightly greased loaf pans (8" x 4" x 2"), and cover with a towel. Let rise for 40 minutes or until nearly doubled in bulk. Preheat the oven to 350°F. Bake for 35 to 45 minutes, or until golden brown and loaves sound hollow when tapped. Cool on racks.

Notes
The bread flour has more protein compared to all-purpose flour in order to counteract the lower protein content in rye flour. This bread is especially scrumptious toasted and topped with chicken salad.

October

Pretzels are an indispensable part of Oktoberfest (page 85), so it's no surprise that October is National Pretzel Month. I love a good stadium pretzel—although there are some pretty bad ones out there, as at some food courts—but recently there has been a surge in the use of pretzel buns for sandwiches. I have used them for tailgate party buffalo chicken sliders, and they do add a certain pizzazz to a backyard burger.

October 9 brings us Submarine-Hoagie-Hero-Grinder Day, the hyphenation being necessary due to regional variations on what to call a sandwich of deli meats and cheeses on an elongated bun. There are other names as well, but a homemade pretzel bun will make it a "hero" no matter what you call it.

Pretzel Buns
1½ cups lukewarm water (about 100°F)
1 package active dry yeast
¼ teaspoon sugar
1½ teaspoons salt
3 tablespoons vegetable oil
4½ cups all-purpose flour
¼ cup baking soda
Pretzel salt, for sprinkling (optional)

In a medium-sized bowl, stir together water, yeast, and sugar, and allow yeast to develop for 5 minutes. Stir in salt and vegetable oil. One cup at a time, add four cups of flour, mixing well between each addition until flour is thoroughly incorporated. Knead for 5 to 8 minutes, adding remaining flour as needed to make a smooth and elastic dough that is only slightly sticky. Lightly oil the surface of the dough, and place it in a clean, dry bowl. Cover with a dry cloth and let rise about an hour or until doubled. Punch the dough down, and knead it lightly.

Line a sheet pan with a silicone baking mat* and set aside. Cut the dough in quarters. Shape each piece of dough into an oval about 5" long. Place them, evenly spaced, on the prepared pan. Cover with a clean dry towel, and allow to rise in a warm place for 15 minutes.

Preheat oven to 400°F. In a large pot or saucepan, bring 2 quarts of water to a low boil. Add the baking soda a little at a time—take your time or it will cause the water to boil over. Lower the heat to a simmer. One or two at a time, poach each roll for 30 seconds, turn it over, and poach for another 30 seconds. Remove with a slotted spoon to the lined sheet pan and sprinkle with pretzel salt if desired. Repeat with the remaining rolls. Using a sharp knife or razor blade, cut three slashes on the top of each roll. Bake rolls for 15 to 20 minutes or until deep brown. Cool, and then slice edgewise to make hero sandwich buns.

*Because of the poaching process used to give them their chewy texture and distinctive shiny brown appearance, pretzels can stick to many pans, even when the surface is coated with pan spray or parchment. A silicone mat is foolproof.

November

Sometime in early November, newspapers, magazines, and websites begin publishing articles about and recipes for cubes of stale bread mixed with herbs, vegetables, and various proteins and anointed with chicken broth. Whether you call it dressing or stuffing depends on where you live (the Butterball® website has a map), but November is officially National Stuffing Month. But that's not the only way to use up stale bread: November 28 is National French Toast Day. Why not combine the two and make Stuffed French Toast?

Stuffed French Toast

2 eggs

½ cup milk

¼ cup granulated sugar

1 teaspoon ground cinnamon

1 teaspoon pure vanilla extract

8 ounces cream cheese, softened

½ cup powdered sugar

2 tablespoons lemon juice

½ cup raspberries,* plus additional berries for garnish

4 thick slices of hearty bread (challah and honey oatmeal both work well)

Combine eggs, milk, sugar, cinnamon, and vanilla extract in a bowl and whisk together. Keep refrigerated until ready to use. Beat cream cheese, powdered sugar, and lemon juice until smooth. Gently fold in raspberries. Preheat oven to 350°F.

Lightly coat a large nonstick skillet with pan spray, and place over medium heat. Dredge the bread in the egg mixture on both sides and place in the pan. Cook until golden brown on both sides, about 2 minutes per side. Remove bread from pan and let cool. Divide filling in half, and then spread on 2 pieces of the bread, then top with the remaining 2 pieces of bread. Transfer to a sheet pan, and bake in the oven for about 8 minutes. To serve, cut each stuffed French toast in half, and serve with syrup or vanilla ice cream. Garnish with fresh berries.

You can use strawberries or blueberries, or take a shortcut by using flavored cream cheese.

December

Long before we started naming national food holidays, December was the month of eggnog and fruitcake. Both can be acquired tastes, the former being too thick and cloying for some people and the latter being, well . . . fruitcake. Before you dismiss this traditional confection too quickly, take the time to go to the local library and check out Truman Capote's "A Christmas Memory," one of the most charming and poignant Christmas stories ever written. Among other themes, the author reminisces on how he baked fruitcakes with his elderly cousin every year. Don't be surprised if you tear up as you read the last page.

If the story doesn't make you buy candied fruit and whiskey, perhaps you'll be inspired instead by National Date Nut Bread Day on December 22. Here's my take, using eggnog as an ingredient—the best of both worlds.

Eggnog Date Nut Bread
2¼ cups all-purpose flour, plus flour for dusting pan
¾ cup granulated sugar
2 teaspoons baking powder
1 teaspoon salt
½ cup chopped pecans
1 cup chopped dates
2 large eggs, beaten
1 cup eggnog
¼ cup vegetable oil

Preheat oven to 350°F. Prepare an 8½" x 4½" loaf pan with pan spray, and dust the sides lightly with flour. Place flour, sugar, baking powder, and salt in a medium-sized bowl, and whisk to combine. Stir in pecans and dates until evenly distributed. In a separate bowl, combine eggs, eggnog, and oil. Add to dry ingredients, mixing just until dry ingredients are moistened—do not overbeat. Pour batter into prepared pan and level. Bake for 70 to 75 minutes, or until a toothpick inserted into the center of the loaf comes out clean. Cool for 10 to 15 minutes before removing from pan to cool the rest of the way on a wire rack. Best if eaten the next day and served with cream cheese.

THIS VS. THAT

Baking Soda vs. Baking Powder

Beginner bakers are often confused as to the difference between baking soda and baking powder. Both are chemical leaveners that release carbon dioxide during the baking process to make baked goods rise, but they cannot be used interchangeably in a recipe.

Baking soda is bicarbonate of soda or sodium bicarbonate. It is used in recipes with some acidic ingredients such as buttermilk, sour cream, vinegar, brown sugar, or lemon juice. The baking soda reacts with the acid to form bubbles of carbon dioxide. Baking soda is powerful and therefore is used in smaller amounts than baking powder, usually one quarter teaspoon per cup of flour in a recipe. If you use too much baking soda, the resulting baked goods often have a bitter or soapy flavor.

Baking powder contains sodium bicarbonate plus cream of tartar along with a little cornstarch. The cream of tartar is the acid that activates the sodium bicarbonate. Some baking powders use sodium aluminum sulfate in place of the cream of tartar. All baking powder should be used at a ratio of one teaspoon per cup of flour.

These chemical leaveners are most often used for quick breads like pancakes, muffins, donuts, and other batter breads. Both baking powder and baking soda lose their potency over time, so be sure to check the expiration date on yours before you begin a recipe (see page 39).

Unsalted Butter vs. Salted Butter

Up until the 1960s, most recipes in the United States called simply for "butter" because almost all butter in the stores was salted, since salt is a preservative and gives the product a longer shelf life. As more Americans became exposed to French cooking thanks to Julia Child and the celebrity chefs who followed her, the unsalted butter more commonly used in Europe began making an appearance in American cookbooks and then in dairy cases. Since different brands of butter may be saltier than others, using unsalted butter means that you have greater control over the amount of salt in a recipe. One should definitely use unsalted butter if a recipe calls for it, or the result may not have the flavor the recipe writer intended. If salted butter is all you have on hand, reduce the amount of salt in the recipe by half. If the recipe simply calls for "butter," then salted butter is usually meant.

Table Salt vs. Kosher Salt vs. Sea Salt

Everyone knows that salt is an important or even essential seasoning for many foods, and most bread recipes call for it. Salt accentuates the flavors of baked goods, and, in yeast breads, it strengthens the gluten matrix and helps yield a lighter crumb. But what kind of salt to use: table, kosher, or sea salt? They have virtually the same chemical composition, but each of them has a unique density and texture.

Table salt comes from mining salt deposits and has fine, evenly shaped crystals. It has greater density than other salts, and often has additives such as calcium silicate (an anti-clumping agent) and iodine (a nutrient that helps prevent goiters). As its name suggests, it's most often used as a last-minute seasoning at the table. When a recipe calls simply for "salt," table salt is what is usually meant.

Kosher salt became more common in the United States after the wave of Eastern European immigrants arrived in the early 1900s, who used this coarse salt to remove blood from the meat they served at home, thereby making it kosher. In the late 1960s, it began to be popular with chefs as a cooking ingredient because its coarse grains were slow to dissolve and added a light crunch. It's an excellent salt for seasoning meats before cooking. It also comes in a finer grain, which many bakers prefer over table salt.

Sea salt is produced by evaporating sea water, and since each body of water has a unique blend of trace elements, each sea salt has a unique flavor, although the differences are often subtle. It tends to be more expensive and is best used as a finishing seasoning for a dish.

So which is best for baking? Very few chefs recommend sea salt for baking (in part because of its cost), and at least one commentator says that kosher salt owes some of its current popularity to food television: kosher salt's coarse grains show up better on camera. In a sweet muffin or a baguette, you might not be able to discern much of a difference between table salt, kosher salt, or sea salt. Just one cautionary note: if a recipe uses kosher salt, and table salt is all you have on hand, remember that table salt is denser and a smaller amount should be used. For example, if 1¼ teaspoons of coarse kosher salt are called for, only 1 teaspoon of table salt would be needed.

Skim Milk vs. Whole Milk vs. Buttermilk

Many bread recipes include milk among the ingredients, especially in breads like cinnamon rolls and other sweet breads with a soft texture and a tender crumb. In older recipes, "milk" always means whole milk, but now that 2% and skim milk are more commonly found in the family fridge, which milk should you use?

In most test kitchens and professional bakeries, whole milk is the default choice because the higher fat content (between 3.5% and 4%) serves to tenderize the crumb of breads and rolls and keep them moist. You can use 2% milk to yield similar results, but skim milk has no fat content, and although it will contribute to the browning of the crust, it will have little effect on the texture of the bread. So if a recipe doesn't specify the fat content of the milk, whole or 2% milk will serve best.

Buttermilk is a slightly sour dairy product that, despite its name, contains no butter. Originally it was the by-product of the process of butter-making. After the cream was churned and the butter had formed, the remaining liquid was the "buttermilk." Today, almost all buttermilk sold in stores is a cultured product made from whole or low-fat milk. It's produced with a lactic-acid bacteria culture that thickens it up and also gives buttermilk its distinct tang. It's often used in quick bread recipes like biscuits and pancakes that include baking soda, which reacts with the acidic buttermilk to create a light and fluffy texture.

Olive Oil vs. Canola Oil

Oils that are liquid at room temperature are generally healthier than other fats like butter or shortening, as the former contains less saturated fat. Canola oil is the healthier of the two, and it has a more neutral flavor, so many bakers prefer it over olive oil or other vegetable oils made from corn or peanuts. But olive oil is a traditional ingredient in many Mediterranean recipes for breads and even some cookies, and the shelves at your local grocery will have a bewildering variety of options—how to choose?

Extra virgin olive oil (EVOO) is made from the first pressing of the olives and is the least processed olive oil, but the strength of its flavor can vary from one brand to the next, and it is the most expensive version of olive oil. I tend to think of EVOO as a condiment—use it sparingly for dressings, drizzle it lightly on pasta, or swirl it on a small plate with some balsamic vinegar and dip your bread into it.

Virgin olive oil is made by the same process as EVOO but from riper olives and has a slightly less intense flavor. It's not commonly found in grocery stores.

Pure olive oil is a blend of virgin olive oil and refined olive oil (heat and/or chemicals are used to extract the oil) and has a more neutral flavor and a lower price. It doesn't have all the health benefits of EVOO but is better for you than solid fats. If a recipe calls for olive oil without specifying, this is the one you should choose.

Light olive oil is a refined oil with a lighter color and flavor—"light" in this case does not refer to calories. It has a higher smoke point than other olive oils and therefore can be used for sautéing and frying.

Shortening vs. Butter

Butter and shortening have vastly different effects in cookies. Cookies made with butter spread out more and are flatter, but are more flavorful than cookies made with shortening. Cookies made with shortening rise taller and are more tender, but do not taste as rich and flavorful.

However, in the case of bread recipes, the difference is not only one of flavor but also moisture content. Butter is about 20% water, and shortening is pure fat, so adjustments in the amount of flour may need to be made when switching from one to the other. Remember also that butter is usually salted, and shortening is not, so substituting the latter for butter may result in a flat-tasting loaf. In addition, substituting shortening for butter in batter breads and other quick breads can result in heavier, denser products unless the shortening is thoroughly creamed with the sugar until light and fluffy before mixing in other ingredients.

Fresh Herbs vs. Dried Herbs

Having an herb garden just outside the kitchen door is a great delight, and a profusion of fresh herbs can be an inspiration to any chef. But if you lack space for such a garden or live where winters are cold and harsh, dried herbs are a necessity. Fresh herbs are available in the produce section of many grocery stores, but there's a limited variety, and they are relatively expensive. So how to convert a recipe from fresh to dried herbs or vice versa? The rule of thumb is three portions of fresh herbs to one portion of dried. For example, if a recipe calls for a tablespoon of freshly minced basil, a teaspoon of dried basil is the rough equivalent.

There are some exceptions to this rule. A fresh bay leaf is replaced by only two dried, and dried sage and thyme are so potent that somewhat less can be used. Most chefs agree that dried parsley and dried chives have such a bland flavor that they are hardly worth the effort, especially since fresh parsley is generally available year-round, and chives can be replaced by the tops of green onions. Fresh garlic is also available in the produce section, but a clove of garlic can be replaced by ¼ teaspoon of granulated garlic.

Remember that dried herbs should be kept in a cool, dark place like a kitchen cabinet rather than on the shelf above the stove where the heat causes them to lose their potency more quickly. Dried herbs have a shelf life of about one year, so marking a purchase date on the container can help you keep track of which seasonings need to be replaced.

Buy the Fresh Garlic!

Nearly every chef uses plenty of garlic, and for most bread recipes, powdered and granulated garlic are acceptable substitutes for fresh. But there's really nothing better than fresh minced garlic in a recipe, especially when you're cooking in a skillet or stockpot. Look in the produce section for unblemished bulbs with papery skins and no soft spots.

Fortunately, whole garlic bulbs have a long shelf life, as long as they're stored in a cool, dry place. Unless you use garlic every day, one bulb at a time should be plenty between trips to the grocery store. If the cloves get soft or shriveled it's time to buy more fresh, and avoid using cloves with green sprouts because they tend to be bitter.

Minced garlic in jars may be convenient, but it also has a bland flavor and not nearly as much nutritional value, and it tends to burn easily in the sauté pan. Don't bother with containers of peeled cloves in the refrigerated case because garlic loses its flavor when it's chilled. Peeling the individual cloves can be frustrating, but most chefs crush the cloves with the flat of a wide chef's knife to loosen the skins for easy peeling. The crushed cloves are easier to mince too.

After you're finished with meal prep, clean your hands and your cutting board with a lemon wedge—the juice neutralizes the odors like magic!

Rolled Oats vs. Quick Oats vs. Steel-Cut Oats

Oats are a popular addition to many breads, and honey oatmeal bread is one of the most popular recipes in my repertoire, both with my fellow monks and my Breadhead followers. But there are several forms of oatmeal available—what are the differences?

Whole, unbroken oat grains are called **groats,** which are usually lightly roasted before being processed into another form, which gives them better flavor and increases their shelf life. They are more often used for hot cereal than for bread baking because the whole grains don't incorporate well into the dough without being soaked or cooked for some time.

Steel-cut oats (also known as Scottish or Irish oats) are groats that have been cut into two or several pieces. They are also commonly used for porridge, but steel-cut oats can be incorporated into a batter bread or kneaded yeast bread if they have been soaked in water overnight or cooked on the stove for at least 30 minutes, and they contribute a nutty, earthy flavor and texture.

Rolled oats (also called "old-fashioned oats") are whole groats that have been steamed and then rolled flat into irregular oval disks. Rolled oats cook faster than steel-cut oats, and for most oatmeal bread recipes, you can simply soak them in hot water for 10 or 15 minutes before use.

Quick cooking rolled oats are cut into smaller pieces, so they soften even faster but they don't contribute as much texture to bread. **Instant oats** are not recommended for oat bread recipes. The pieces are steamed longer and cut even smaller, making it the most processed form of oats. Instant oatmeal often has additional ingredients like artificial flavoring, oat flour, caramel color, and salt.

Cooking Spray vs. Parchment Paper vs. Silicone Mats

A stoneware deck oven is naturally nonstick, but ever since the invention of metal pans, bakers have been trying to figure out how to keep bread from sticking to them. Even so-called nonstick pans sometimes need a little assistance for certain recipes, batter breads and muffins being among the chief examples.

Cooking spray is an update of the earlier method of smearing a pan with grease, oil, or butter. Cooking spray is inexpensive and does a decent job, although some cheaper brands tend to burn at higher temps or with longer cooking times. It's especially convenient for muffin tins, loaf pans, and cake pans, or any baking vessels with an odd shape or multiple angles. Some batter bread recipes call for dusting the pan with a layer of flour after spraying, and baking spray with flour added is available. Its primary drawback is that pans require more cleanup, and it darkens pans after repeated use.

Parchment paper has gained greater popularity in recent years and can now be found in most grocery stores in a roll similar to plastic wrap or foil. It's used to line sheet pans and jelly roll pans for cookies, flatbreads like focaccia, and braided, round/oval, or free-form loaves. Parchment is convenient in that it can be cut to any size of pan, is easy to store, and is simply thrown away after use—a genuine advantage when you are baking in large numbers. Cookies and breads baked on parchment have a browner, crisper crust than those baked on silicone. However, some people are bothered by the waste and by the expense of having to keep buying it. When used off a roll, it sometimes refuses to lie flat, but it is also available in packages of flat sheets. Serious Breadheads buy bulk packs of large parchment sheets from restaurant supply companies and cut them to fit.

Silicone mats are made of fiberglass coated with food-grade silicone. They are completely nonstick without the addition of oil or baking spray, and they can be washed and reused thousands of times (one manufacturer claims 3,000 uses). They are relatively expensive—$20 to $30 each, depending on the brand—but since they can be used over and over, they are economical if you bake often. Some people recommend that you replace them yearly if you bake several times a week. I use mine for any recipe that is especially sticky, like a braided coffee cake with a filling that might ooze out onto the pan, and for peanut brittle and other hard candies. They are also the most reliable surface on which to bake pretzels or bagels that have undergone a hot water bath before baking. They come in a limited number of sizes, so make sure you buy one that matches the dimensions of the pan you intend to use. Cutting them to fit is not recommended because that would expose the fiberglass filaments inside the silicone.

Dark Pans vs. Light Pans vs. Insulated Pans

Most of us buy our baking pans one or two at a time, adding to our collection as we have need of more jelly roll pans for a big batch of Christmas cookies or a specialty pan for a new recipe. Pans tend to darken with use, especially if we're not too careful about scrubbing all the dark spots off a shiny new pan. As a result, experienced bakers have pans in a variety of shades, from shiny silver to muddy brown and even some that are blackened with years of use.

Darker materials and bread pans typically absorb and radiate more heat. A dark pan is the best choice if you want breads with a darker crust (pizza is a great example). A more delicate batter bread is better off in a pan with a lighter color. Braided, round, or free-form loaves can be baked on a cookie sheet or jelly roll pan of any color, but you may need to experiment with baking times and temperatures to get the desired results. With a shiny pan, raising the temperature of the oven 25°F will help you achieve a browner crust if that's what you want. In the same way, lowering the temp 25°F. will keep crusts from browning too much in a darker pan.

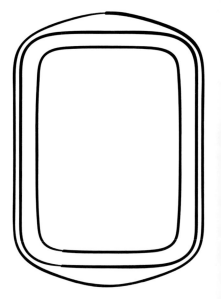

Insulated cookie sheets are ideal for preventing delicate cookies (like spritz) from browning too quickly. I don't recommend them for most breads, although I occasionally use them for small breads like hamburger buns or rich dough with a lot of sugar, like Danish pastries.

Secrets of My Bookshelf

W henever I visit friends' kitchens, I always want to take a peek at what cookbooks are on the shelf within easy reach. What's their go-to cookbook for family dinners? Do they bake bread, pies, cakes, cookies, or all of them? Are they a fan of Betty Crocker or the Barefoot Contessa? And, I must confess—are any of my books in their collection? Sometimes I discover a new treasure worth putting on an Amazon wish list or a vintage cookbook to pursue in secondhand bookstores and flea markets.

This might lead you to ask: What's on *your* bookshelf, Fr. Dom? As you might imagine, I have a sizable collection of bread books, but not all of them make the kitchen shelf, and some are even more carefully enshrined in my monastery room. So here's a brief annotated bibliography of my favorites: the ones that have especially inspired me or get the most use. You can find lists of the latest best sellers online—some of these are a little harder to find.

I received my first cookbook on my ninth birthday, October 25, 1969: *The Pooh Cook Book* by Virginia H. Ellison. Winnie-the-Pooh has been a dear friend since I got a Pooh puppet for Christmas at age four. It had a music box inside that played Brahms's "Lullaby" when you pulled the string. When the music box failed, my mom removed it and turned the puppet into a doll with legs. I have it still, and it's propped up on the shelf next to the book. I remember tying on a too-big apron and making Honey Buns and Blueberry Muffins from these recipes, and one of these days, I'll get around to making Cottleston Pie too. "Ask me a riddle, and I'll reply. . . ."

Another fine source of literary-inspired recipes is *The Little House Cookbook* by Barbara M. Walker, with recipes based on the "Little House on the Prairie" stories by Laura Ingalls Wilder. My sister gave me that

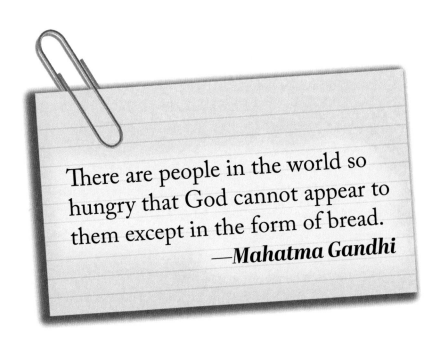

There are people in the world so hungry that God cannot appear to them except in the form of bread.
—*Mahatma Gandhi*

book for Christmas in 2000. Pick it up and you'll learn a lot about American pioneer cooking in the 1800s. I enjoy making the corn dodgers recipe on page 23. *The Food Journal of Lewis & Clark: Recipes for an Expedition* by Mary Gunderson is fascinating as well, and it inspired me to make sourdough biscuits on the 200th anniversary of Sacagawea making them when the Corps of Discovery reached the Pacific. I was blessed to meet the delightful author and get a signed copy.

I do love a good history book, and I have two outstanding examples on my Breadhead bookshelf. The first is *Six Thousand Years of Bread: Its Holy and Unholy History* by H. E. Jacob, first published in 1943. He traces the role of bread through civilization, starting with the ancient Egyptians, farming in biblical times, the role of bread in Christianity, the famines of the Middle Ages, and the shortsighted greed and mismanagement that led to the French Revolution. *The History of Bread* by Bernard Dupaigne traces the same history, but this coffee-table-sized book is lavishly illustrated with full-color photos and illustrations. Jacob's book is more scholarly, while Dupaigne's is a more popular treatment of the subject. Both make for delicious reading.

The other treasure in my monastery room is Robert Farrar Capon's *The Supper of the Lamb,* a culinary reflection on food that is equal parts Christian spirituality and gastronomic gusto. Capon spends a whole chapter meticulously describing the dissection of an onion, not as a botanist, but as a man who believes in God but also loves a good roast. Later in the book, you'll learn things as diverse as how a roux thickens sauces, what puts the puff in pastry, how to cook in a wok, and detailed instructions on how to host a proper dinner party without making yourself crazy. This was the book that taught me that a wavy bread knife is superior to a serrated one, and which offers this nugget of bread wisdom: "A woman with her sleeves rolled up and flour on her hands is one of the most glorious stabilities in the world. Don't let your family miss the sight." Capon wrote that in 1967—today I would hope he'd include men in the picture as well! I cannot recommend this book highly enough. I reread it every year, but I have an extra copy you can borrow.

Then there are my kitchen shelves. Tucked away in the locked pantry of the abbey kitchen are the shelves with my special pans, pizza equipment (including the hot sausage herb mix from DiGregorio's on the Hill in St. Louis), a bottle of good Mexican vanilla, and the workhorse bread books in my collection. These are the ones that I use most often, with tattered or missing dust jackets, dented corners, and stained pages. The entire kitchen staff knows these books are off-limits, although I once had to track down my 1962 edition of *The Joy of Cooking* when Fr. Gabriel "borrowed" it for a dinner party.

The 1975 edition of Irma Rombauer's *The Joy of Cooking* is considered among the best, and I know you can buy everything online these days, but let me just say that the excitement of finding a vintage cookbook you've been wanting for some time for two bucks at a rummage sale will produce far more satisfaction than free shipping. I've bought dozens of copies of *Joy* at secondhand shops and antique malls, and I've never paid more than $12, sometimes as little as $4. I give them away as door prizes at my bread demos. Sure, the new edition has recipes that reflect more contemporary tastes—but it would be hard to improve on the 1955 directions for *pâte à choux*.

The Better Homes and Gardens Bread Cook Book is another out-of-print treasure that shows up regularly at Goodwill stores and flea markets. First published in 1963, it went through four printings and was in kitchens all over America. Look for cinnamon swirl bread and a Swedish tea ring on the cover. You could spend four months baking your way just through the breakfast breads for your Sunday mornings. It has helpful photos of techniques throughout, so you can learn a lot about shaping dough if you manage to score a copy.

If you're looking for photos that inspire rather than inform, *Ultimate Bread* belongs in your collection. Eric Treuille and Ursula Ferrigno's oversized cookbook looks like it belongs on your coffee table along with *Style* magazine and the latest *Travel+Leisure*. The recipes are eclectic and internationally diverse, but the photos are glorious (Treuille is a food stylist and it shows). Thanks to this book, I know how to make French *fougasse*, Portuguese *bolo rei*, and Victorian milk bread.

Bernard Clayton Jr.'s *The Complete Book of Breads* has more than 200 recipes in it. My 1973 copy was found at a garage sale by Mary Ellen,

a dear family friend of happy memory, who inscribed it: "I'll take a half dozen of each!" This tome and *The Joy of Cooking* might be all you need to become an accomplished baker and cook. I honed my beginner's baking skills by following Clayton's detailed but easy-to-follow instructions accompanied by little stories of how he came by the recipes. A new edition with 300 recipes came out in 2003, with revisions to reflect the rise of bread machines and instant yeast—and I have that one too.

I learned most of what I know about sourdough from Ed Wood's **Classic Sourdoughs: A Home Baker's Handbook**, and **Sourdough Jack's Cookery** by Jack Mabee. Wood is a microbiologist-turned-historian-and-baker who managed to reproduce the method by which the first leavened breads were baked in Egypt. Mabee was a chuck wagon cook in Alaska whose modest comb-bound recipe book taught me the delights of sourdough pinch-off biscuits baked in a cast-iron skillet. Wood operates a website where you can purchase sourdough starters from around the world.

If I'm in the mood for baking sweet treats rather than savory breads, I pull out *The Back in the Day Bakery Cookbook*. Forget *Southern Living's* website—brother and sister team Cheryl and Griffith Day are my muses. The recipe titles alone are enough to make me wash my hands and get out the mixer: Pinkies Chocolate Lunchbox Treats, Bourbon Pecan Pie, 'Nana Puddin', Almond Crunchies, and Bacon-Jam Empanadas. And Chapter 7: Brownies and Bars—epic.

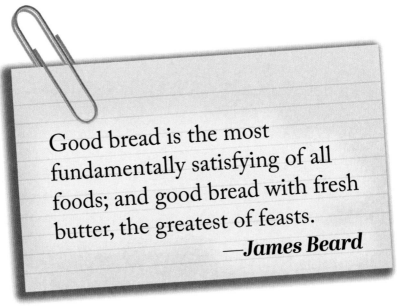

Good bread is the most fundamentally satisfying of all foods; and good bread with fresh butter, the greatest of feasts.

—*James Beard*

Speaking of sweets, I have and highly recommend Shirley O. Corriher's *BakeWise: The Hows and Whys of Successful Baking*. A follow-up to her equally engaging *CookWise*, this sizable volume on the art and science of baking concentrates more on cakes and quick breads than on yeast breads, but it's a fascinating read. She tells you *how* to make moist cakes that never fall, the flakiest pie crusts, and the crustiest baguettes, but also *why* the techniques work the way they do. Buy it just for her Improved Tunnel of Fudge Cake—you can thank me later.

If you scan my bookshelf too quickly, you could easily miss *The Cornbread Book: A Love Story with Recipes* by Jeremy Jackson. It's a slim volume that could fit in an apron pocket but is packed with delicious cornmeal recipes and good humor. His Creamed Cornbread recipe is a favorite of Abbot Philip. *The Cornbread Gospels* by the delightfully-named Crescent Dragonwagon is a more substantial book for the serious cornbread lover from either side of the Mason-Dixon Line. She packs the book with sidebars and asides that are both entertaining and educational. As a man who loves cornbread so much that as a child I would ask for it instead of birthday cake, I always keep these books within easy reach.

My most recent acquisition is *A Blessing of Bread: Recipes and Rituals, Memories and Mitzvahs* by Maggie Glezer. My mother was "gleaning," as she put it: working to reduce clutter on her bookshelf. I received a stack of bread books, including best sellers *Crust* by Richard Bertinet and *Flour Water Salt Yeast* by Ken Forkish, but Glezer's cookbook was the *real* treasure. Her first book on artisan baking won a 2000 James Beard Foundation Award, but in the first chapter of this 2008 book, I learned more about the method and meaning of Jewish baking than I've learned in the past 15 years. If you like challah, babka, and bagels, you'd better look this one up.

There are other books on the secret pantry shelves: *Homemade Bread* by the editors of *Farm Journal*, Mariana Honig's *Breads of the World*, and just about everything written by Peter Reinhart, as well as a half-dozen parish cookbooks with recipes for Monkey Bread, Grandma's Dinner Rolls, Lemon Lush, and the like. I get suggestions from Pinterest on shaping techniques and posts on my Facebook feed for the latest "BEST BREAD EVER—just three ingredients!" Fr. Ronald tears pizza recipes out of *Food and Wine* and leaves them in my mailbox as a hint. I do not lack for recipes. With the Internet, nobody does.

But I say it all the time: people don't need recipes—they need *reasons* to bake. Ultimately, that's why these books are treasures. It's not the clear instructions or the helpful illustrations of technique (although those help) that get me into the abbey kitchen. It's the book with the charming backstory to each recipe, the old-fashioned methods, the photo of a classic loaf on a breadboard, bathed in the light streaming through a kitchen window. It's the book with the recipe named after a beloved grandmother or called by a name in another language that was once spoken in your family, or a bread that uses leftovers creatively so that abundance never turns into waste and from thence to carelessness and ingratitude. It's the book with the tattered cover and the stained pages that falls open to the page with a once-untried recipe that became a family favorite.

And that's the *real* secret in the baker's kitchen. If you don't have such a book, find one soon.

My Irish ancestors on my mother's side had a song to accompany any task that was repetitive: hauling in the nets, sweeping the floor, grinding grain, and, I suspect, kneading dough. I was unable to find such a song, so I decided to write one for myself. It is sung, of course, to the rhythm of the kneading itself—fold, push, and turn, fold, push, and turn—so you can choose your own speed. The tune lends itself to humming as well.

Kneading Song

Bread for the rich man at his ta - ble,
Bread for the poor man in the street.
Bread for the old and bread for the chil - dren,
Bread is the food that all may eat.
Made for the chil - dren by their moth - er,
Made by the hus - band for his wife;
Made by the Lord to feed five thou - sand;
Je - sus is the Bread of Life.

Index

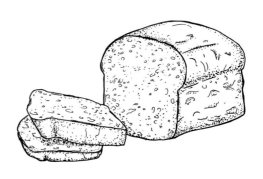

Other Books
by Father Dominic

Breaking Bread with Father Dominic

Breaking Bread with Father Dominic II

More Breaking Bread

Bake and Be Blessed

'Tis the Season to Be Baking:
Christmas Reflections and Bread Recipes

Brother Jerome and the Angels in the Bakery

Thursday Night Pizza:
Father Dominic's Favorite Pizza Recipes

How to Be a Breadhead:
A Beginner's Guide to Baking

The Breadhead Bible:
Father Dominic's Favorite Recipes

Baking Your Way Through the Holidays: Breads,
Cakes & Treats for All Your Celebrations

Breakfast Breads & Sweet Treats